Understanding Diseases and Disorders

AIDS

Sudipta Bardhan-Quallen

KIDHAVEN PRESS

An imprint of Thomson Gale, a part of The Thomson Corporation

THOMSON
TM
GALE

Detroit • New York • San Francisco • San Diego • New Haven, Conn.
Waterville, Maine • London • Munich

THOMSON
™
GALE

© 2005 Thomson Gale, a part of The Thomson Corporation.

Thomson and Star Logo are trademarks and Gale and KidHaven Press are registered trademarks used herein under license.

For more information, contact
KidHaven Press
27500 Drake Rd.
Farmington Hills, MI 48331-3535
Or you can visit our Internet site at http://www.gale.com

LIBRARY OF CONGRESS CATALOGING-IN-PUBLICATION DATA

Bardhan-Quallen, Sudipta.
    AIDS / by Sudipta Bardhan-Quallen.
        p. cm. — (Understanding diseases and disorders)
    Simultaneously published: San Diego, Calif. : Lucent Books, 2004
    Includes bibliographical references and index.
    Contents: What is AIDS?—What is HIV and how does it spread?—Treating HIV and AIDS—Living with HIV and AIDS.
    ISBN 0-7377-2638-5 (hardcover : alk. paper)
    1. AIDS (Disease)—Juvenile literature. I. Title. II. Series.
    RC606.65.B37 2005
    616.97'92—dc22
                                                          2004023003

Printed in the United States of America

Contents

Chapter One

What Is AIDS?

AIDS **(acquired immune deficiency syndrome)** is a serious problem around the world. In 2003 the United Nations estimated that 42 million people globally were living with **HIV (human immunodeficiency virus)** disease or AIDS. Approximately sixteen thousand new infections take place each day. Around half of all people with HIV become infected before the age of twenty-five and die from AIDS before age thirty-five.

In the early years of the AIDS epidemic the great majority of people with AIDS were homosexual men or intravenous drug users (people who inject drugs directly into their veins). People did not think AIDS would spread to the rest of the population.

As time went on, however, it became clear that HIV could infect anyone, regardless of age, sex, race, social status, or location. In fact by 2004 women and children made up the majority of HIV and AIDS cases worldwide.

Although anyone can contract HIV, AIDS affects the poorest nations of the world more than developed nations like the United States. Experts estimate that fewer than 1 million people in the United States have HIV disease or AIDS, whereas in Africa over 28 million people do.

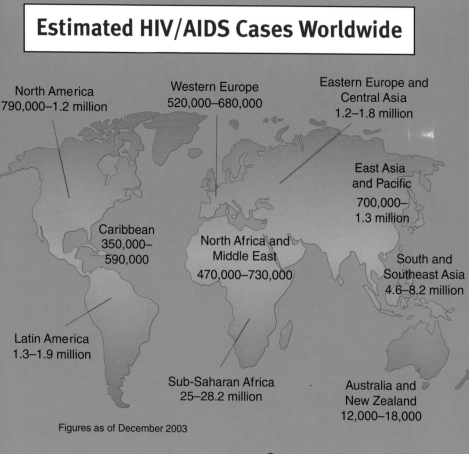

Estimated HIV/AIDS Cases Worldwide

North America
790,000–1.2 million

Western Europe
520,000–680,000

Eastern Europe and
Central Asia
1.2–1.8 million

East Asia
and Pacific
700,000–
1.3 million

Caribbean
350,000–
590,000

North Africa and
Middle East
470,000–730,000

South and
Southeast Asia
4.6–8.2 million

Latin America
1.3–1.9 million

Sub-Saharan Africa
25–28.2 million

Australia and
New Zealand
12,000–18,000

Figures as of December 2003

Source: www.avert.org/worldstats.htm

AIDS and Infections

When the human body gets an infection the immune system is responsible for healing the body. Sometimes, however, infections can themselves

The marks on this man's face and neck are symptoms of Kaposi's sarcoma, a cancer commonly seen in AIDS patients.

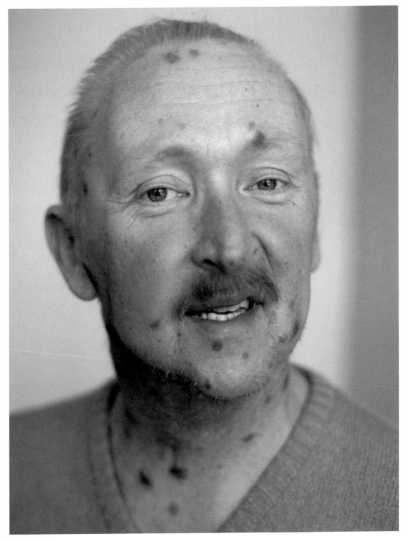

interfere with or damage the immune system and its ability to heal. In those cases the body is left open to dangerous new infections. One disease that is especially successful in damaging the immune system is called AIDS.

In healthy people the immune system is made up of many types of specialized cells. For example, cells called **killer T cells** kill certain types of cancerous tumor cells. **Helper T cells** and **B cells** work together to produce **proteins**, called **antibodies**, that attack specific infections. In people with AIDS, however, helper T cells are singled out and damaged by the disease. Over time patients with AIDS lose great numbers of helper T cells, which limits their bodies' ability to make antibodies. Without antibodies a body cannot fight infections.

One of the well-known **characteristics** of AIDS is that people who have it suffer from a lot of infections. Often these infections are rare in healthy people and sometimes are actually more common to animals such as sheep, goats, and cats than humans. Because patients with AIDS have damaged immune systems, infections that would not normally be able to take hold in the body can, and do. These infections are called **opportunistic infections**.

One of the earliest patients to be diagnosed with AIDS was Margrethe Rask, a doctor from Denmark who had been working in Zaire in the 1970s. Rask became extremely ill in 1976 with swollen lymph nodes, fatigue, and trouble breathing. As she lay dying in a Copenhagen hospital, Rask was diagnosed with **Pneumocystis carinii pneumonia** (a rare pneumonia), **yeast infections** of the mouth, and **Staphylococcus aureus infections**. Each of these infections is treatable. Yet Rask's body could not fight them, and they eventually resulted in her death. Doctors now know that the infections Rask suffered from are common features of AIDS.

Other common opportunistic infections seen in patients who have AIDS are **Kaposi's sarcoma** (a rare and normally harmless skin cancer usually seen only in older men), **toxoplasmosis**, and **cytomegalovirus (CMV)** infections. Patients may experience one or many of these opportunistic infections, and doctors have no way to predict which infections will strike.

Ryan White was a boy who had AIDS in the 1980s. He suffered through many opportunistic infections. He described some of his symptoms in his autobiography:

> I had chronic diarrhea. . . . I got it from a parasite that your digestive tract usually kills off for you—unless you have AIDS. Same with my pneumonia—it was a very unusual kind that mostly hits AIDS patients. . . . I developed funny-tasting white patches [from a yeast infection] inside my mouth. . . . I also had herpes in my throat, which made it incredibly sore—far worse than any normal sore throat.[1]

Diagnosed with AIDS at the age of thirteen, Ryan White suffered through many infections during his short life.

What Causes AIDS?

Patients who have AIDS are actually at the final stage of their battle with the microorganism that causes AIDS, the virus called HIV. When HIV infects a person's body, it begins to damage the immune system.

Since there is no known cure for HIV, doctors can only slow the damage caused by HIV by using powerful drugs.

Before 1983, doctors and scientists did not know anything about HIV—not even that it existed. Between 1983 and 1984, scientists in France and in the United States discovered HIV and proved that it caused AIDS. They also designed a blood test that could detect whether a person was infected with HIV. If a patient's HIV test comes back positive, he or she is considered HIV-positive. These patients are also considered to have HIV disease, which, without treatment, will eventually become AIDS.

What Does HIV Disease Do to People?

In the final stage of HIV disease when a patient has full-blown AIDS, he or she contracts many opportunistic infections that ravage the body and cause death. Long before a patient suffers through these diseases, he or she may notice a number of milder symptoms.

Immediately following infection with HIV, people generally do not show any symptoms of disease. The virus begins by copying itself over and over again. This first phase of HIV disease is called the **window period**. The window period can last between four weeks and six months, and people can transmit HIV to others during this time.

When the window period is over, the patient's body begins to produce large quantities of virus. He or she experiences symptoms similar to the flu, including fever, fatigue, diarrhea, rash, mild muscle

Concerned that she may have HIV disease, a woman talks with her doctor about AIDS.

aches, and headaches. Often people completely over-look these symptoms because they are mild. This stage, called **acute infection**, lasts only between one and two weeks.

Eventually the patient's immune system is able to gain control over HIV. The patient then enters **clinical latency** and is free of harmful symptoms. Clinical latency can last up to twenty years without treatment, although the average period is between two and fifteen years. Unfortunately HIV is able to hide inside certain tissues of the body and never completely goes away. Instead the virus lies in wait, sometimes for years. It continually damages the immune system as it copies itself.

A woman with AIDS is hospitalized after her immune system became too weak to fight off infections.

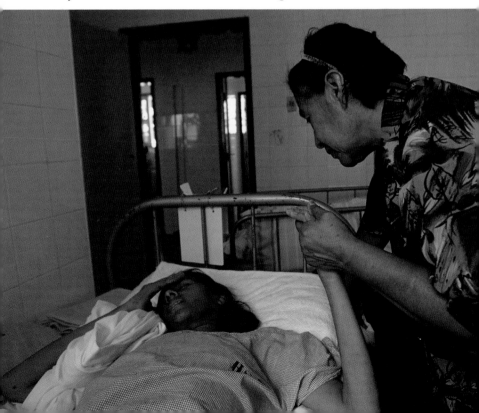

At some point, though, HIV begins to defeat the immune system. The patient then may begin to suffer from symptoms including fever, skin rashes, tiredness, weight loss, or night sweats. These symptoms occur because the immune system is no longer able to protect the patient from infections.

Within two to three years of the beginning of these minor symptoms the patient is likely to develop full-blown AIDS. A patient has AIDS when either the number of helper T cells in his or her blood drops way below normal, or he or she has at least one opportunistic infection.

People with AIDS face serious medical problems. Fortunately doctors know how people can protect themselves from becoming infected with HIV. Education about HIV can help control the spread of this disease. In fact, though scientists think that 45 million more people will have HIV disease by 2010, they also estimate that 29 million of these cases can be avoided through effective HIV education and prevention.

Chapter Two

What Is HIV and How Does It Spread?

Scientists do not yet know why AIDS progresses differently in different people. Doctors cannot predict how quickly a particular patient will become sick and how severe his or her symptoms will be. For example, some people develop AIDS within one year of contracting HIV, whereas others have no symptoms for fifteen years. One thing that scientists do know, however, is that AIDS is caused by HIV. Every person who is diagnosed with AIDS also tests positive for HIV.

Because HIV is a virus, it is difficult to treat. Unlike bacterial infections, viral infections cannot be cured by antibiotics. Viruses cannot be eliminated from the patient's body with medicines. Doctors can only treat the symptoms. The immune system must destroy virus-infected cells in order to end the infection.

The flu is a common disease also caused by a virus. When a person gets the flu, the flu virus infects the person's cells, and he or she suffers through flu symptoms for a while. As soon as the immune system is able to destroy all the cells that the flu virus has infected, the patient is cured.

With HIV, however, the virus attacks the very cells—helper T cells—responsible for helping the

This image, magnified many times, shows a white blood cell (orange) infected with HIV (blue).

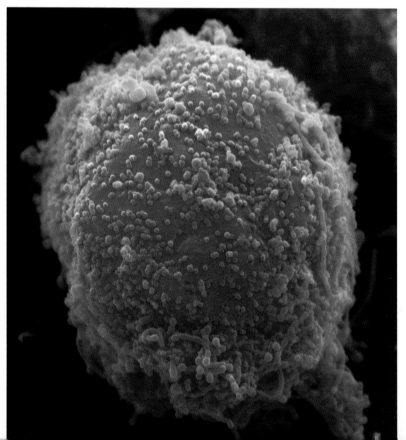

immune system eliminate the infection. Over several months or several years, depending on the patient, the body eventually loses too many T cells. It is unable to combat any type of infection. At this point opportunistic infections begin.

Fortunately for most people, it is very difficult to contract HIV unless they come in direct contact with infected bodily fluids, such as blood, breast milk, or semen. Unlike the flu, HIV cannot be caught by being in the same room as a sick person. In fact, the only way to contract HIV is through contact with HIV-infected blood, through sexual contact with a person living with HIV, or through contact between a pregnant or nursing mother and her child.

Sexual Contact Can Spread HIV

As of 2004 the most common way to become infected with HIV is through sexual contact with an individual living with HIV. A person can become infected through any type of sexual contact, and infection can occur with just one exposure.

When Lizzie Porter was seventeen years old she had a sexual encounter with a man infected with HIV. They did not use a condom, and Porter did not even worry that her actions might lead to contracting HIV. She explained, "My mom stressed no babies and no drugs, but we never talked about AIDS. If I had known about it, I would have been more careful."[2]

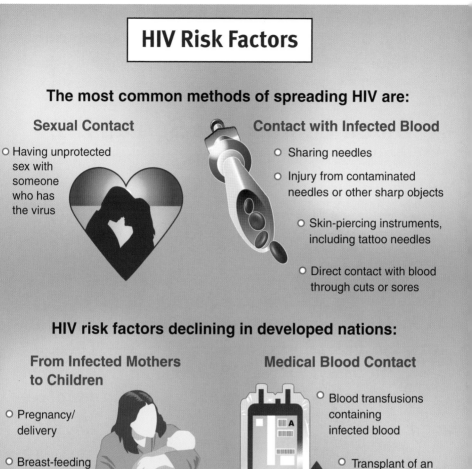

HIV Risk Factors

The most common methods of spreading HIV are:

Sexual Contact

O Having unprotected sex with someone who has the virus

Contact with Infected Blood

O Sharing needles

O Injury from contaminated needles or other sharp objects

O Skin-piercing instruments, including tattoo needles

O Direct contact with blood through cuts or sores

HIV risk factors declining in developed nations:

From Infected Mothers to Children

O Pregnancy/ delivery

O Breast-feeding

Medical Blood Contact

O Blood transfusions containing infected blood

O Transplant of an infected organ

DeShala Thompson contracted HIV from her boyfriend when she was also seventeen years old. She was planning to marry him, so she did not practice safe sex. "We had unprotected sex. . . . He knew he had it [HIV], but he didn't tell me."[3]

As with other forms of HIV transmission, doctors know how to prevent the virus from spreading through sexual contact. When people use condoms, the risk is greatly reduced. Researchers are also developing new ointments called microbicides. These can be used during intercourse to kill HIV particles before they can infect anyone.

Blood Contact Can Spread HIV

Blood contact, such as through a blood transfusion, is a very common way of transmitting HIV. In fact, in the United States, thousands of people contracted HIV in the 1980s from HIV-infected blood or blood products. One such person was Ryan White. Ryan had hemophilia, a disease that causes blood to not clot properly on its own. He needed injections of factor VIII, which is purified from normal blood, to make his blood clot in case of an injury. Some of the factor VIII he received, however, was tainted with HIV. As Ryan described, "what had been keeping me well had given me AIDS, drop by drop."[4]

When scientists realized that HIV was present in the blood supply, blood screening for HIV was used to prevent new infections from tainted blood. Currently there is almost no risk of contracting HIV from a blood transfusion in the United States because the blood supply is extensively screened. Not all countries of the world, however, screen blood for HIV. For example, in 2001 tens of thousands of villagers in China's Henan Province contracted HIV because they were unknowingly given infected blood.

Transfusions are not the only form of blood contact that can spread HIV. Infected blood from a reused hypodermic needle can also spread the virus. People who inject drugs into their veins (called intravenous, or IV, drug users) and who share needles with others are at great risk for contracting HIV. They have no way of knowing whether the other people who have used the needle are infected with HIV. Also medical professionals face the risk of

In the 1980s many people in the United States contracted HIV through blood that was infected with the virus.

being accidentally stuck with a contaminated needle and contracting HIV, although this is rare.

Simple measures can prevent the spread of HIV through blood contact. Screening the blood supply often by testing it for HIV is one safety measure. Medical professionals must also use latex gloves. The use of clean needles, both in medical settings and by IV drug users, prevents HIV from passing from one person to another.

HIV Can Be Spread from Mother to Child

Most children with HIV disease contract the virus from an infected mother. During pregnancy HIV

A doctor examines an African baby for signs of HIV. Millions of African children contract the virus from their mothers.

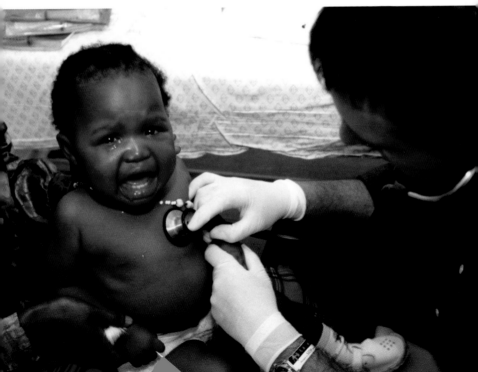

can be transmitted to a fetus through the placenta, the tissue that provides it with oxygen, water, and nutrients from the mother's blood. The disease can also be transmitted during delivery, when babies may come into contact with their mothers' blood. Approximately six hundred thousand infants are born with HIV each year worldwide.

Breast-feeding also poses a risk for spreading HIV from mother to child. Breast milk of infected mothers contains a high concentration of HIV. When babies drink HIV-infected breast milk, they can be infected. In fact, breast-feeding doubles the chances of HIV infection being passed from mother to child.

Scientists know how to prevent the spread of HIV from mothers to their children. Women who take anti-HIV medicines such as AZT during pregnancy greatly reduce the risk of infecting their babies. Women who have tested positive for HIV are also cautioned against breast-feeding their infants. Unfortunately, in many underdeveloped areas of the world proper medicines and advice are often unavailable. In addition, mothers usually cannot afford to buy formula or milk to feed their infants.

Nkosi Johnson was a boy in Africa who contracted HIV from his mother at birth. When he was eleven years old Johnson described what it was like to have AIDS. In a speech at the thirteenth International AIDS Conference in 2001 he said, "I

Nkosi Johnson, who died of AIDS at the age of twelve, shares his story at the 2001 International AIDS Conference.

hate having AIDS because I get very sick and I get very sad when I think of all the other children and babies that are sick with AIDS. I just wish that the government can start giving AZT [an anti-HIV drug] to pregnant HIV mothers to help stop the virus being passed on to their babies."[5]

Casual Contact Cannot Spread HIV

One thing that is very clear is that casual contact—including hugging, using the same toilets or chairs, and shaking hands with a person who has HIV—does not spread the virus. Casual contact does not give HIV an opportunity to enter another person's body, so infection cannot occur.

Because casual contact between infected and uninfected people is safe, a person with HIV can enjoy a normal life. A person who has HIV is able to work, take care of children, exercise—do almost anything that a healthy person can do. As Johnson said in his 2001 speech, "I want people to understand about AIDS—to be careful and respect AIDS—you can't get AIDS if you touch, hug, kiss, hold hands with someone who is infected. Care for us and accept us—we are all human beings. We are normal. We have hands. We have feet. We can walk, we can talk, we have needs just like everyone else—don't be afraid of us."[6]

Chapter Three

Treating HIV and AIDS

There is no known cure for HIV disease. The goal in treating HIV disease is to control the virus and its effects on the body. Fortunately drugs are available that slow HIV's ability to damage the immune system. These medicines can delay the beginning of full-blown AIDS, sometimes by years. The most common drug regimen is **highly active antiretroviral therapy**, or **HAART**. HAART combines different types of anti-HIV medicines. The combination is much more powerful than the individual drugs.

HAART: Combination Therapy

The main anti-HIV drugs are called **reverse transcriptase inhibitors** and **protease inhibitors**. Both types of drugs prevent the virus from making more copies of itself. In a typical HAART treatment a patient is given three or four different anti-HIV drugs at once.

When it works HAART adds decades to patients' lives. For example, Dan Cusick was told in July 1995 that AIDS would end his life by October. Cusick began HAART as a last-ditch effort. The drugs worked. Within a few weeks Cusick's symptoms began to disappear, and doctors could no longer find even a trace of HIV in his blood. Linda Grinberg had HIV-related yeast infections, CMV, and extreme fatigue. Her doctors placed her on HAART, which changed her life. She said, "It's

Although there is no cure for HIV, certain drugs can help delay the onset of full-blown AIDS.

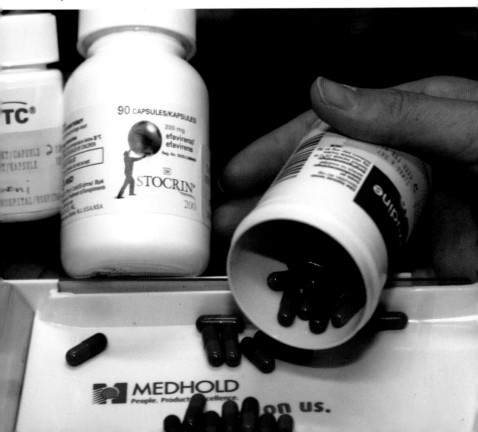

A South African health worker teaches a patient with HIV how to combine the pills of her HAART regimen.

given me back my life. A year ago, it was difficult even to get dressed. I really felt I was at the end of the line."[7] After Grinberg received HAART, her infections disappeared, and she could again live her life in a normal way.

Taking HAART, however, can be very complicated. Often patients must take a large number of pills at regular time intervals. If a patient misses even a single dose, he or she runs the risk of developing **drug resistance**. A patient is considered to have developed drug resistance when the drugs he or she is taking no longer damage the HIV in his or her body. When drug resistance occurs, patients can quickly become sick again from HIV.

Scientists have realized that HAART sometimes fails simply because the patient does not take the medications correctly. Said Denise McDowell, director of the HIV charity the George House Trust, in 2001: "We have got to recognize that it's very hard to change your lifestyle to fit the very complex regimes that many anti-HIV drugs require. It is vital that doctors do not just dispense medication without spending time with people to work out which therapies and life changes are possible."[8]

Another problem with HAART is that the side effects of the drugs can make people very sick. Patients can have headaches, nausea, anemia, abdominal pain or discomfort, or diarrhea. HAART can sometimes damage the patient's liver, nerves, bone marrow, kidneys, and pancreas. Any of these side effects can also become life threatening and sometimes can force a patient to stop HAART.

Janie's HIV Treatments

Janie Queen is a child in North Carolina who is HIV-positive. She was infected with HIV at birth and then given up for adoption. Her adoptive family helps Janie cope with having HIV disease and the challenges in treating it.

Janie takes twenty pills and three teaspoons of medicine every day. Anytime someone in her family leaves the house they yell, "Janie, take your medicine!"[9] The reminders are important since, in Janie's words, "if you don't take it [the medicines] at the right time, you'll get sick and die."[10] Every three months Janie must fly from her home in North Carolina to Houston, Texas, to be examined by doctors at Texas Children's Hospital. So far this routine has kept Janie healthy. HIV is barely detectable in her blood.

Every morning Janie begins her drug regimen at 6:45 with a squirt of a cherry-flavored reverse transcriptase inhibitor, ddI. At school she visits the nurse's office at 8:00 A.M. where she gets seven pills: six large pills of a protease inhibitor called saquinavir and one small capsule of a different reverse transcriptase inhibitor, d4T.

Before Janie leaves school at 2:45 P.M., she visits the nurse again for six more saquinavir pills. After dinner she gets another squirt of ddI. Long after her bedtime, at 11:00 P.M., her mother wakes her to take seven more pills, the same ones as in her 8:00 A.M. dose.

Janie's treatments cost much more than one thousand dollars a month. She is lucky: Her family's insurance company pays much of the cost, and the hospital covers many of the fees. Still, the treatments are necessary. Because of HAART Janie's life is fairly normal, and she is healthy and active.

Other Treatments for HIV and AIDS

HAART drugs are often very expensive. People with HIV living in poor areas can seldom afford the medicines they need. This, in addition to the number of patients who become extremely sick from the side effects of HAART, has made scientists search for new treatments.

In the opinion of many experts, a **vaccine** is the best hope for containing the spread of HIV disease. As Sam Avrett, the associate scientific director of the International AIDS Vaccine Initiative (IAVI),

HIV-positive children in Kenya take a liquid reverse transcriptase inhibitor as part of their daily dose of medication.

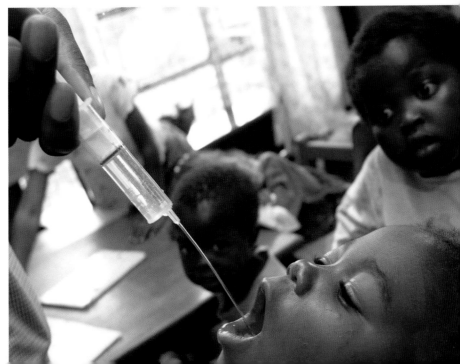

explained, "Vaccine research is critical because a vaccine is one of the best foreseeable ways to control the AIDS epidemic, both in the U.S. and around the world. . . . Although behavior change [like practicing safe sex and using clean needles] can do a lot, it is just not realistic to expect individual behavior change, by itself, to control this epidemic."[11]

A vaccine is injected into the body to cause it to produce an immune response. Often a vaccine is given during childhood to protect a person from disease for his or her entire lifetime. Vaccines can also be used to treat a disease after someone becomes sick. An HIV vaccine could prevent HIV infection and treat people who already have HIV disease.

Medical researchers all over the world, like this woman in Germany, are working to develop an HIV vaccine.

Despite the many years of research into HIV vaccines, as of 2004 a working vaccine had not been developed.

While the vaccine research continues, scientists are also developing new anti-HIV drugs. For example, a new class of HIV inhibitor, called **entry inhibitors**, has been developed. These drugs prevent HIV from infecting T cells even after the virus is inside a person's body. Doctors hope that entry inhibitors will strengthen current HAART treatments. The first entry inhibitor, a drug called Fuzeon, is so powerful against HIV that many patients see a 90 percent drop in viral levels. Unfortunately, Fuzeon is very expensive. The yearly cost is estimated to be around twenty thousand dollars, far more than any other HAART drug. This high cost means that people living with HIV in developing nations have little hope of affording this drug. Experts are hopeful that over time the cost of Fuzeon and other entry inhibitors will fall enough for the drugs to be widely used.

Through the existing drugs and the medicines that scientists hope to develop in the near future, people with HIV are no longer helpless against the disease. Yet there is still a great deal of work to be done to defeat the disease of AIDS. As Secretary of State Colin Powell said in 2001, "I know of no enemy in war more insidious or vicious than AIDS. . . . The war against AIDS has no front lines. We must wage it on every front."[12]

Chapter Four

Living with HIV and AIDS

When HIV and AIDS were first discovered, doctors had no way to treat their patients with HIV disease. With research and new medicines, said Dr. Patrick Morrow, HIV disease "is no longer a death sentence, and, with proper management, every one of our HIV patients can live a normal and full life."[13]

HIV Education Prevents Discrimination

People with HIV disease must take care of their own health to maintain a good quality of life. Just as important, however, is that people learn about HIV disease and AIDS to make sure that people with HIV are not discriminated against. Discrimination can make life for HIV patients just as difficult as the disease itself.

When the AIDS epidemic began in the 1980s, many people did not understand how a person got AIDS or HIV. A number of myths began to spread: HIV could be transmitted by using public restrooms, taking elevators, or by "sharing a bologna sandwich"[14] with someone who already had HIV. These myths created a difficult environment for HIV patients. Some parents kept their children out of school because they feared there might be children with HIV in a class. Many patients diagnosed early in the epidemic were fired from their jobs, turned out of their homes, and sometimes denied adequate health care, even in hospitals.

As HIV disease was better understood, scientists and doctors in the United States and Europe began

Kept from attending school, AIDS patient Ryan White participates in his math class over the telephone.

to better educate the public. Over time a great deal of the discrimination in developed nations against people with HIV disease has decreased. In poorer developing nations such as Africa and Asia, however, HIV patients are still singled out for discrimination. For example, Tamil is a woman with HIV in India. She became infected with the virus through her husband. When she found out she had HIV, she felt ashamed. In 2003 Tamil said, "I didn't tell anybody that I had the virus. I told them [her family] at the time that it was jaundice because I was afraid of the stigma and discrimination."[15]

This discrimination prevents many people from being tested for HIV since they do not want to face shame if their community finds out that they have HIV. These people sometimes continue to pass HIV to others. The lack of education creates difficulties for people living with HIV and for efforts to stop the spread of the virus.

Keeping Communities Aware

Though people with HIV are more likely to face discrimination in developing nations, in truth, discrimination can happen in any community, especially when other people do not know the facts about HIV. For example, when Sandra Queen tried to enroll Janie, her daughter who has HIV, in day care, no day care center would take her. They were all afraid that having her in the facility would endanger the other children and caregivers. When Janie was in

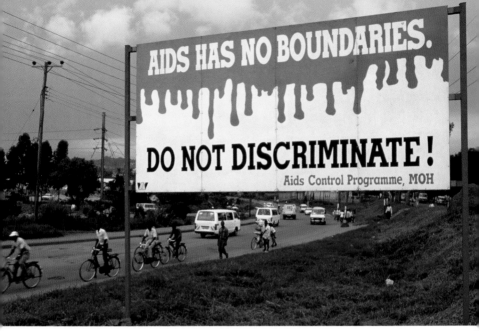

Discrimination against people with HIV is a problem in developing nations, as this sign in Uganda shows.

the first grade, a pregnant teacher quit her job rather than have Janie in her class.

On the other hand, many members of Janie's community were willing to learn about HIV disease so that Janie could have a normal childhood. Queen routinely trains her daughter's teachers, babysitters, and coaches to use latex gloves if Janie has an emergency. If they do not have gloves available, Queen instructs them to wad up a T-shirt or towel, and then to wash their hands thoroughly afterward. By informing the community, the Queens have created an environment that is pleasant and comfortable for Janie while also being safe for everyone else. In addition, the HIV education that the Queens are giving their community may prevent their friends and neighbors from contracting HIV themselves.

Living with HIV and AIDS

Making Medicines Available to Everyone

Because Janie and her family are knowledgeable about HIV and AIDS, she is able to have a comfortable life even with HIV. Unfortunately, the vast majority of people with HIV disease live in areas of the world where they do not have access to medicines to keep them healthy. In many countries massive AIDS epidemics are underway. This disease takes not only the lives of its victims, but it ravages the victims' communities as well. Approximately 80 percent of the people infected with HIV are between twenty and fifty years old, which is also the portion of society that is usually

A Global View of AIDS

- An estimated 42 million people are living with HIV/AIDS. Of these, 37 million are adults and 2.5 million are children under fifteen.

- Approximately 5 million people became infected with HIV in 2003. This includes 4.2 million adults and 700,000 children under fifteen.

- AIDS caused the deaths of an estimated 3 million people in 2003. This includes 2.5 million adults and 500,000 children under fifteen.

- AIDS drugs extend lives, but they do not cure HIV or AIDS.

Figures as of December 2003

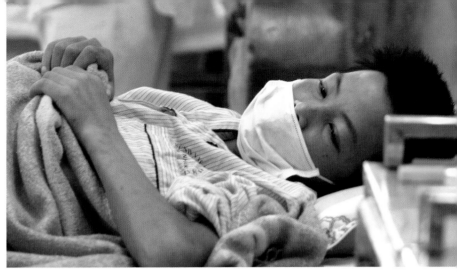

A young AIDS patient receives costly anti-HIV drug treatment in a Vietnamese hospital.

responsible for earning money and raising children. As these people sicken and die, the impact on their communities is enormous. As former president Bill Clinton described,

> In some nations, teachers, doctors, and nurses are dying faster than they can be trained. . . . Farmers and farm laborers are dying, cutting food production. . . . Police and military personnel dying undermines public order and safety. And most important, the mothers and fathers dying in droves undermines the fabric of families, social life, and civilization itself. [16]

The main thing that prevents these people from getting the necessary anti-HIV medicines is money. In most of the developing world, people with HIV disease simply cannot afford expensive HAART drugs. In fact, as of 2003 only four hundred thousand

In 2004 demonstrators in Thailand demand that anti-HIV medicines be made available to everyone.

people in developing countries had access to lifesaving anti-HIV drugs, even though the total number of people living with HIV was well over 30 million.

Many **humanitarian** and scientific organizations are working to make medicines available to everyone who needs them. Though it will be difficult, many people hope that scientists will find a cure for HIV disease in the twenty-first century. Said United Nations secretary-general Kofi Annan in 2001,

> No continent, no society, and no social group is immune from this scourge. . . . Adolescents and children are dying every day, and in every country. So are their parents—young adults in what should be the prime of their lives. But action is possible. Despair is not justified, for we are not powerless against this epidemic. We can beat this disease.[17]

Notes

Chapter 1: What Is AIDS?

1. Ryan White and Marie Cunningham, *My Own Story*. New York: Signet, 1992, pp. 72–73.

Chapter 2: What Is HIV and How Does It Spread?

2. Quoted in Dahleen Glanton, "Emerging Face of HIV," *Chicago Tribune,* March 28, 2004. www.chicagotribune.com.
3. Quoted in Glanton, "Emerging Face of HIV."
4. White and Cunningham, *My Own Story,* p. 61.
5. Nkosi Johnson, "Care for Us and Accept Us, We Are All Human Beings," remarks as delivered at the Thirteenth International AIDS Conference, January 9, 2001. http://nkosi.iafrica. com/speech.
6. Johnson, "Care for Us and Accept Us."

Chapter 3: Treating HIV and AIDS

7. Quoted in Christine Gorman, "A New Attack on AIDS," *Time,* July 8, 1996. www.time.com.
8. Quoted in *BBC News,* "HIV Drugs Misused," September 10, 2001. http://news.bbc.co.uk.

9. Quoted in Lea Hopper, "Worlds Apart: Heaven Can Wait," *Houston Chronicle,* 1999. www.chron.com/content/chronicle/special/99/hiv/janiecover.html.

10. Quoted in Hopper, "Worlds Apart: Heaven Can Wait."

11. Quoted in John S. James, "HIV Vaccines Need to Be Developed: Interview with Sam Avrett, International AIDS Vaccine Initiative," *AIDS Treatment News,* May 1, 1997. www.aids.org.

12. Colin Powell, "Address at United Nations Special Session on HIV/AIDS," remarks as delivered to the United Nations General Assembly, June 25, 2001. www.state.gov/secretary/rm/2001/3756.htm.

Chapter 4: Living with HIV and AIDS

13. Quoted in Cindy McCanse, "HIV Infection: No Longer a Death Sentence," *FP Report,* October 2000. www.aafp.org/fpr.

14. Quoted in Jerry Adler, "The AIDS Conflict," *Newsweek,* September 23, 1985. www.msnbc.msn.com.

15. Quoted in *BBC News,* "Living with HIV: Voices from Around the Globe—'I Had No-One,'" December 3, 2003. http://news.bbc.co.uk.

16. Bill Clinton, remarks as delivered at the Tenth Conference on Retroviruses and Opportunistic Infections, February 10, 2003. www.clinton presidentialcenter.com/retroviral_2003.html.

17. Kofi Annan, "How the World Can Win Its Battle Against AIDS," *New York Times,* June 25, 2001. www.un.org/News/ossg/sg/stories/sg_aids.htm.

Glossary

acquired immune deficiency syndrome (AIDS): A disease that damages the immune system and leaves the body open to life-threatening infections.

acute infection: The stage of HIV disease when large quantities of HIV are produced, but the person's immune system has not yet begun to fight the infection with antibodies.

antibodies: Proteins that help the immune system attack specific infections.

B cells: Immune cells that make antibodies with the aid of helper T cells.

characteristics: Distinguishing features.

clinical latency: The period of HIV disease where the patient experiences few, if any, harmful symptoms.

cytomegalovirus (CMV): A viral infection that is normally harmless but that can cause serious health complications in patients who have HIV.

drug resistance: Occurs when an infection is no longer treatable by drugs that had worked in the past.

entry inhibitors: Anti-HIV drugs that block the virus's ability to infect new cells.

helper T cells: Immune cells that help B cells make antibodies.

highly active antiretroviral therapy (HAART): A combination of different HIV inhibitor drugs that is very effective in controlling HIV disease.

human immunodeficiency virus (HIV): The virus that causes AIDS.

humanitarian: Actions that help other people.

Kaposi's sarcoma: A rare cancer often seen in patients diagnosed with HIV.

killer T cells: Immune cells that kill certain kinds of cancerous tumor cells and virus-infected cells.

opportunistic infections: Infections that occur when the immune system is damaged.

Pneumocystis carinii pneumonia: A severe type of pneumonia, common to patients with HIV.

protease inhibitors: Anti-HIV drugs that prevent HIV from copying itself.

proteins: Molecules used by living things.

reverse transcriptase inhibitors: A type of anti-HIV drug that prevents HIV from copying itself.

Staphylococcus aureus infection: Bacterial infections commonly found in patients with HIV.

toxoplasmosis: An infection often seen in HIV patients.

vaccine: A substance that causes the body to produce an immune response, which can often protect a person from disease.

window period: The period between infection by HIV and the beginning of antibody production by the body.

yeast infection: Overgrowth of microorganisms usually found in the body. Occurs commonly in patients with HIV and causes health problems.

For Further Exploration

Books

Gustav Mark Gedatus, *HIV and AIDS*. Mankato: MN: Capstone, 1999. An easy-to-read discussion of all aspects of HIV disease.

Daniel Jussim, *AIDS & HIV: Risky Business*. Berkeley Heights, NJ: Enslow, 1997. An overview of the history of AIDS and anti-HIV treatments.

Ben Sonder, *Epidemic of Silence: The Facts About Women and AIDS*. New York: Franklin Watts, 1999. Discusses the issues around HIV disease in women and how different approaches must be taken to protect women from infection.

Gail B. Stewart, *People with AIDS*. San Diego: Lucent, 1996. Presents personal accounts of people living with HIV or AIDS.

Conrad J. Storad, *Inside AIDS: HIV Attacks the Immune System*. Minneapolis: Lerner, 1998. A scientific discussion of the effects of HIV on the immune system.

Compiled by Lori S. Weiner, Aprille Best, and Philip A. Pizzo, *Be a Friend: Children Who Live with HIV Speak*. Morton Grove, IL: Albert Whitman, 1994. A collection of the stories of children aged five through nineteen who are HIV-positive.

Ryan White and Marie Cunningham, *My Own Story.* New York: Signet, 1992. Ryan's personal account of living with HIV and AIDS.

Web Sites

American Foundation for AIDS Research (amFAR) (www.amfar.org). The amFAR Web site provides basic information about HIV and AIDS; presents news regarding scientific discoveries, treatment options, and public policy issues; and provides information about HIV and AIDS conferences.

AVERT (www.avert.org). AVERT is a United Kingdom–based HIV and AIDS charity. Its Web site covers a great deal of information about the history of AIDS, HIV transmission, treatment of the disease, and education materials. There are specific sections devoted to the world epidemic and to personal stories of people with HIV.

The Body (www.thebody.org). This comprehensive Web site provides articles on every aspect of HIV disease, from basic information, to treatment options, to ways to support AIDS research. It also presents the latest AIDS-related news stories.

International AIDS Trust (www.aidstrust.org). The International AIDS Trust was established to help world governments and nongovernmental organizations direct their efforts in partnership to find solutions to the problems caused by AIDS.

Joint United Nations Programme on HIV/AIDS (UNAIDS) (www.unaids.org). UNAIDS is a global advocate for HIV treatment and research. On this Web site visitors can find statistics about HIV and AIDS, information about what is being done around the world, and proposals for dealing with the crisis in the future.

National Association of People with AIDS (NAPWA) (www.napwa.org). This Web site provides details about different AIDS advocacy programs, aimed at ensuring that people with AIDS are given the same rights and treatment as uninfected people. There is also information about AIDS treatments and how to finance them.

Index